# Paddleboard Guide to Lake Tahoe

*Circle Lake Tahoe in 24 Paddles*

**LAURA NORMAN**

SUP GUIDES

SAN FRANCISCO, CA

SUP Guides
109 Hoffman Ave
San Francisco, CA 94114
www.tahoesupguide.com

Publisher's Note: While every effort has been taken to ensure the accuracy of this guide, the publisher cannot accept responsibility for errors or changes over time.

Paddleboard Guide to Lake Tahoe/ Laura Norman. -- 1st ed.
ISBN 978-1-63192-897-0

*With thanks to Hilary Craddock, Jennifer Maeder, Julia Reiff, and Killian Higgins who joined me for various stages of the journey, and to Michael Raneri for paddling some of the legs with me and watching our kids while I finished the others. Many friends have also contributed to this book. I am grateful to Tom Stahl and Elizabeth Kain for helping with the writing, and Gerry Rodriguez with graphics. And special thanks to Keep Tahoe Blue and all the people that dedicate their time to preserving this beautiful lake.*

# Contents

# Introduction

Within my first five minutes of stepping onto a stand up paddleboard on Lake Tahoe, I was hooked. The second deepest lake in the United States has turquoise water, giant boulders, and snow-capped mountains in every direction. There's really no other place like it to paddle in in the world.

After spending a summer paddling near our home on the west shore, I decided it would be a fun challenge to try to paddle the entire perimeter of the lake. A leisurely two years later I finished, after visiting every single beach along Lake Tahoe's 72-mile shoreline and trying every possible launching spot.

While working my way around the lake, I discovered that there weren't any resources that explained how to circumnavigate it. Paddleboarders have unique needs that aren't addressed by kayaking guides. We are more affected by wind, waves, and motorboat traffic. And we typically can't go as far in a day. This particular paddleboarder can only carry her board a short distance from the car and prefers launch spots with public restrooms. A nearby coffee shop is also a plus. Since I've photographed each paddle and described it for my blog, a guidebook seemed like the next logical step.

This book describes how to circumnavigate the lake in 24 paddles. If you want to do the whole lake, just follow the paddles sequentially until you've gone all the way around. Many of the paddles can be reversed because you can just as easily start from one end as the other. (Sometimes that's not possible so you may be jumping ahead and paddling "backwards" to link up.) All but one are "there and back." You can always turn back early if you want to go a shorter distance on a given day. For planning purposes, you can estimate 30-40 minutes per mile.

If you are a beginner and just want to test the waters, you can rent a board at some of the more popular beaches. If you don't own a board of your own but want to check out some of the other spots, you can rent a board and strap it on top of your car. (In some places you can even have a board delivered.) If you only have a day or two in the area and want to find the most scenic paddles, this book can also help. There are also a couple of day-long, one-way paddles for people who want a big adventure.

I've rated every paddle between 1 and 4 stars, but it was difficult not to give them all a 4. Wherever you decide to go on Lake Tahoe, you're sure to have a great time.

*A note: To the best of my knowledge the information in this book is correct, but there's no guarantee that if you visit a destination that there will be a parking spot readily available or that the port-a-potty will still be there. (Or that it will be clean). And, with California's drought situation, the landscape is continuing to change. This I can guarantee: It's always better to go as early as possible in the morning (the wind often kicks up in Tahoe by 11 am in the mornings). It's also better to go on a weekday. If you are planning to paddle on a weekend or holiday, try to go extra early and avoid the busier beaches where there is the most boat traffic. The most beautiful paddles on Lake Tahoe are generally the most difficult to get to, but they are all worth the effort.*

# Lake Tahoe Map

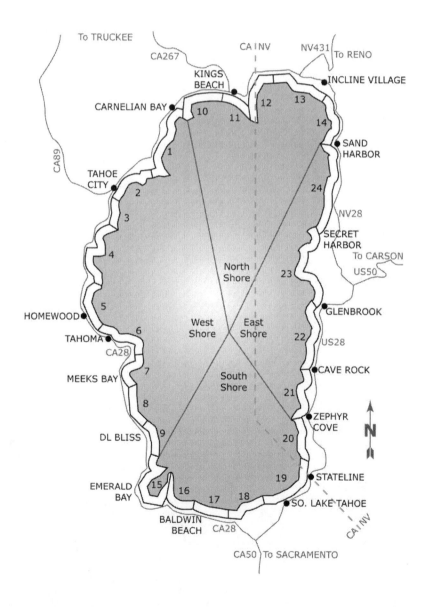

# Numbered paddles

**West Shore**
1. Carnelian Bay to Lake Forest Beach
2. Lake Forest Beach to Commons Beach
3. Commons Beach to Sunnyside
4. Sunnyside to Fleur du Lac
5. Obexer's to Chambers Landing
6. Chambers Landing to Sugar Pine Point
7. Meeks Bay to Sugar Pine Point
8. Meeks Bay to D.L. Bliss
9. D.L. Bliss to Emerald Bay

**North Shore**
10. Carnelian Bay to Kings Beach
11. Kings Beach to Speedboat Beach
12. Speedboat Beach to Crystal Bay
13. Incline Beaches
14. Sand Harbor to Incline Village

**South Shore**
15. Emerald Bay
16. Baldwin Beach to Emerald Bay
17. Baldwin Beach to Pope Beach
18. Pope Beach to Connolly Beach
19. Nevada Beach to Connolly Beach

**East Shore**
20. Nevada Beach to Zephyr Cove
21. Zephyr Cove to Cave Rock
22. Cave Rock to Glenbrook
23. Glenbrook to Whale Beach
24. Sand Harbor to Secret Harbor

# 8 Most Scenic Paddles

If you're a paddle enthusiast with a limited amount of time to explore Lake Tahoe, here are eight "can't miss" paddles. If you aren't able to find a rental, you can check with one of the shops mentioned later in the book to reserve a board and load it on your car.

**West Shore**
Meeks Bay to Sugar Pine Point (rentals available)
Meeks Bay to D.L. Bliss State Park (rentals available)

**South Shore**
Emerald Bay (rentals available)
Baldwin Beach to Emerald Bay/D.L. Bliss State Park (rentals available)
Baldwin Beach to Pope Beach (rentals available)

**North Shore**
Speedboat Beach to Crystal Bay

**East Shore**
Sand Harbor to Secret Harbor (rentals available)
Glenbrook to Secret Harbor

# West Shore

The west shore stretches from Carnelian Bay down to Emerald Bay. It's the longest stretch of the lake, with eight paddles to complete, but it has some of the most beautiful and easily accessible routes. There's a lot of development along the west shore with hundreds of homes, multiple marinas (including Sierra Boat Company, Tahoe City Marina, Sunnyside, and Obexer's), and many anchored boats. It's also the home of two of the lake's most beautiful state parks with miles of pristine shoreline. D.L. Bliss is famous for its beautiful cove and high cliffs. And Sugar Pine Point is the lake's best-kept secret, a fantastic park with a long beach and swimming pier.

# 1 - Carnelian Bay to Lake Forest Beach

**Web**: www.watermanslanding.com
**Phone:** (530) 546-3590
**Parking:** free lot, street
**Distance from car:** short
**Bathrooms:** yes
**Rentals:** yes
**Boat traffic:** ok
**Rating:** **
**Length:** 8 miles

One of the most popular places for renting paddle-boards on Lake Tahoe is Waterman's Landing in Carnelian Bay. Although it's not located on one of Tahoe's premier beaches, it's very convenient. There's a rocky beach that's a short walk from your car and easy to launch from, a cafe, and even clean bathrooms. It's also dog friendly. Offering rentals, races, classes, and summer camps, Waterman's has been an enthusiastic promoter of paddleboarding on Lake Tahoe, so it's a fitting place to start your tour of the lake.

You'll often see a lot of beginners renting paddle-boards, but you can also demo expensive boards intended for more experienced paddlers. They run classes and camps in the summer, but are open all year round, and some hardy souls paddle all winter long from their beach. I once went in early March and saw several other cold-weather paddlers leave Waterman's that same day.

If the parking at Waterman's is full, you can also launch from a little beach that's next to Garwoods (a popular north shore restaurant). It has easy parking, a bathroom, and a little grassy area (just watch out for the goose poop.)

Make a right out of the beach at Waterman's, then paddle about four miles to get to Lake Forest Beach. For the first mile or so, the road is fairly close to the shore and you'll pass many West Shore homes. As you pass the Chinquapin development, the road moves away from the shore and it's quieter as you reach Dollar Point. You'll see the Dollar Point Beach Club with many kayaks and paddleboards on the shore and Skylandia Beach (which is not a good launch spot because it is a very long walk from the car, including a steep flight of steps). There are some interesting rock formations along the shore on this side too.

Lake Shore Beach, your turnaround point, is located on Dollar Point, which is a wonderful area because it is removed from the busy road that runs all the way around the lake, and the neighborhoods are quiet and relaxed. This rocky beach is extremely shallow, even in dry years. Sometimes there's a little island there (called "Ghost Island"), but when the lake level is low it becomes part of the shoreline.

(Note: you can just as easily do this paddle by starting at Lake Forest Beach, which is also an easy launch point and described in the next section. If you need to break it into two shorter paddles, go south from Carnelian Bay for two miles, then turn around. For your next paddle, go north from Lake Forest Beach until you reach your turn-around point, about two miles.)

*Dollar Point from Carnelian Bay.*

# 2 - Lake Forest Beach to Commons Beach

**Web:** n/a
**Phone:** n/a
**Parking:** 8-10 spaces, no fees
**Distance from car:** very short
**Bathrooms:** Port-a-potty (sometimes)
**Rentals:** yes
**Boat traffic:** can be bad
**Rating:** *
**Length:** 3 miles

To get to Lake Forest Beach, drive north out of Tahoe City about 2 miles and make a right onto Lakeshore Drive. Make a right onto Bristlecone Road and drive ¼ mile to the beach. It's located on Dollar Point, which is a wonderful area because it is removed from the busy road that runs all the way around the lake, and the neighborhoods are quiet and relaxed. It's very shallow here, so it's not a destination beach and very challenging in dry years, but it has easy parking just steps from the water. This is a great place to launch if you are in the Tahoe City area and want to go for a quick paddle without dealing with the hustle and bustle of Commons Beach. The best paddling is to make a left out of the beach and head for Carnelian Bay, but to link up the lake you need to make a right and head toward Tahoe City.

It's about a mile and a half to paddle to Commons Beach. The water is shallow most of the way and you can clearly see the bottom. It looks like a giant rock slab in some places, which is unique for Tahoe. Otherwise, it's not a particularly interesting paddle, as you pass the parking lot for Safeway, and lots of private docks. This paddle is only recommended if you are trying to link up the lake.

*Tahoe City Marina.*

# 3 - Commons Beach to Sunnyside

**Web:** www.tcpud.org/parksrec/facilities.shtml
**Phone:** (530) 546-1215
**Parking:** 30 free spaces, street
**Distance from car:** short
**Bathrooms:** yes
**Rentals:** yes
**Boat traffic:** Not bad
**Rating:** ***
**Length:** 5 miles

Commons Beach is located in Tahoe City, just north of the "Y." It's one of the most convenient launch spots and one of the best places on the lake for beginners. This little beach has plenty of free parking, a large playground, a grassy play area, and lots of clean bathrooms. It is close to the shops and restaurants of Tahoe City (Syd's Bagelry is a favorite). Tahoe City Kayak also rents paddleboards and kayaks on the beach.

If you're a more advanced paddler, don't let its convenient location or the many small children playing there fool you. This is a great place for a paddle. The only downside is that it is very shallow and can be tricky in dry years. Make a right as you head out of the beach (going left would take you by the Tahoe City Marina and lots of boats). You'll pass the dam which lets water out to the Truckee River and then the pier and private beach of the Tahoe Taverns condos as well as some private homes.

Since the water is shallow, the powerboats are anchored a long way from shore, creating a tranquil corridor for paddling. I've done this paddle many times, and its surprisingly pleasant even on a weekend or holiday morning.

After the corridor, you'll pass a point with a dark boathouse at the end of a pier. Around the point, you'll enter the bay at Sunnyside and see the red, green, and blue umbrellas of the restaurant. It's about 2-1/2 miles to get all the way to Sunnyside, but still a nice paddle if you turn back anywhere along the way.

*Sunnyside.*

# 4 - Sunnyside to Fleur du Lac

**Web:** www.tcpud.org/parksrec/facilities.shtml
**Phone:** (530) 543-2600
**Parking:** 5 free spots, street
**Distance from car:** Short
**Bathrooms:** yes
**Rentals:** yes
**Boat traffic:** can be busy
**Rating:** **
**Length:** 6 miles

Sunnyside/William Kent Shoreline is about 2 miles south by car from Tahoe City. From the road, you will see a few parking spots and a small building (which houses 2 restrooms), located just after the market at Sunnyside and before the marina and restaurant. There are only a couple of parking spots, but if they aren't available you can usually find something on the street.

Because of its proximity to the marina, this paddle is best for a weekday, although you may still encounter water skiers. Make a right as you leave the beach and quickly cross by Sunnyside Marina. You'll pass some nice west shore homes and then the lovely, undeveloped watershed where Ward Creek meets the lake as you turn into Hurricane Bay.

Hurricane Bay is very deep and surprisingly calm. It's a lovely place to paddle and there's a lot of parking and easy access from the road if you want to start your paddle here instead of Sunnyside. Round the point by Elizabeth Williams Park (a small rocky beach that seems to be mostly used for fishing), and continue to Fleur du Lac at the start of McKinney Bay.

Fleur du Lac Estates is a large homeowners association located on the north side of Homewood. It's best known as a setting for the Godfather 2, and from the lake you can see the original estate from the movie as well as a breakwater and yacht club. If you want to keep going, it's another ½ mile to Obexer's Marina.

*Hurricane Bay.*

# 5 – Obexer's to Chambers Landing

**Web:** www.obexersboat.com
**Phone:** (530) 525-7962
**Parking:** street
**Distance from car:** short
**Bathrooms:** in the general store
**Rentals:** yes
**Boat traffic:** can be busy
**Rating:** *
**Length:** 5 miles

This paddle covers the distance between Obexer's Marina (located by Homewood, South of Tahoe City) and Chambers Landing, but you also need to circle a mile back to Fleur du Lac if you want to link up the entire lake. Although Obexer's is a very easy place to launch from, it is a marina and there can be a lot of boat traffic. This paddle is only recommended if you are trying to link up the entire lake. (If you are merely looking for a nice paddle in the area, drive a couple of miles further south and paddle from Chambers Landing to Sugar Pine Point). To launch your paddleboard, drive into the marina, unload your board and carry it to the beach on the north side of the marina where the sailing school keeps its boats. Then park your car out on the street. Otherwise it is a long carry.

To link up with the other paddles, you'll need to make a left out of the beach and paddle past the moored boats to Fleur du Lac (approximately 1 mile). Then turn back and paddle past Obexer's to Chamber's Landing (a little bar at the end of a pier) which is a mile south of the marina.

The nice thing about paddling at Obexer's is the general store and snack bar that you can hit at the end.

# 6 - Chambers Landing to Sugar Pine Point

**Web:** n/a
**Phone:** (530) 543-2600
**Parking:** 20 free spots
**Distance from car:** short
**Bathrooms:** port-a-potties
**Rentals:** no
**Boat traffic:** not bad
**Rating:** ***
**Length:** 4 miles

This is one of the best launch spots on the west shore, but it's not at all obvious from the road. Chambers Landing looks like a private beach, and although there is a private club there, there's also a little public beach (no bathrooms, only port-a-potties). There's a zone for unloading your car and you can generally find parking except on busy weekends or holidays. The only downside is that it's a shallow, rocky beach so like Lake Forest and Commons Beach, it can be challenging in dry years. But even if it's difficult to get into the water, it's always worth it. I've done this paddle in all types of weather in almost every season, and it never disappoints.

Make a right out of the beach and paddle past the Tahoma condos and homes. After a mile you'll be at the start of Sugar Pine Point State Park, and the rest of the paddle will be alongside the undeveloped shoreline of the park. There are a lot of big rocks in the water along the shore, so keep an eye out for shallow ones. It's easy to hit them if you are close in or if the water is low. After about a mile you'll reach the point at the north end of Sugar Pine Point beach. There's a big marker on the shore and a lot of rocks in the water. Turn around here for a shorter paddle or continue down the full length of Sugar Pine Point.

The beach is about a mile long. It's one of the most beautiful places on the lake with a long pier and turquoise water. First you'll pass the "boat beach" where boaters like to camp, and then the pier and the lawn of the Erhman Mansion, and then a long rocky beach. It's a 4 mile paddle if you turn around on the north side of Sugar Pine Point, 6 miles to the far end of the beach and back.

Because Sugar Pine Point sticks far out into the lake, boats going north and south along the west shore typically pass close by, so there can sometimes be a lot of boat chop here, but it is very unpredictable. Sometimes it is very rough on a Saturday afternoon, but other times it is quite calm. What is predictable is how beautiful Sugar Pine Point is.

(A note about Sugar Pine Point:  This is one of the lake's best kept secrets. Maybe it's because you can't see the beach from the lake, or because you have to walk a long way from the parking lot to the beach, or because the state charges $10 for parking, but even on holiday weekends it doesn't sell out. You can rent paddleboards on the beach, but it's not advised to bring your own unless you have wheels because it's a very, very long way to the water from your car.)

*North end of Sugar Pine Point.*

# 7 - Meeks Bay to Sugar Pine Point

**Web:** www.meeksbayresort.com
**Phone:** (530) 525-6946
**Parking:** hundreds of spaces, $10 fee
**Distance from car:** short
**Bathrooms:** port-a-potties
**Rentals:** yes
**Boat traffic:** not bad
**Rating:** ****
**Length:** 2-4 miles

The only way to paddle out of Sugar Pine Point is to rent a board at the boathouse. (Rentals are available on the Sugar Pine Point beach from West Shore Sports.) The beach is too far from the parking lot for anyone to carry their own board down to the beach. If you are using your own board, it's easier to start at Meeks Bay and paddle back up to Sugar Pine Point to link up the lake.

Meeks Bay Resort (the private section of Meeks Bay) is very easy to paddle from. You can get in as early as 7 in the morning — even if the gatehouse is not staffed, you can pay the $10 parking fee in the office. This is a fantastic time to paddle. There's an easy place to drop off equipment and there's tons of parking. (I don't think it fills up, even on holidays). The beach can get extremely crowded in the summer, but the turquoise water is always gorgeous. There is a marina, though, so you will get boat traffic on busy days although it's not as bad as some of the other marinas. There are lots of port-a-potties at Meeks Bay Resort. And there's a snack bar and a general store if you want something to eat. (There is also a State Park at Meeks Bay, but I've always paddled out of the resort because my family likes the snack bar.)

*South end of Sugar Pine Point.*

Make a left and paddle north as you leave the beach. There's a little cove at the north end of Meek's Bay and a house on the point. After that, you'll pass a few private homes and then the forested south end of Sugar Pine Point. Paddle up to the southernmost point and then make a left and continue along the beach to your turnaround point from Chamber's Landing. The beach at Sugar Pine is at least a mile long, so depending on where you turned around coming from Chambers Landing, you can have a good 3-4 mile paddle from Meeks. It can be very, very choppy at the point later in the day but this is a gorgeous paddle.

# 8 - Meeks Bay to D.L. Bliss

**Web:** www.meeksbayresort.com
**Phone:** (530) 525-6946
**Parking:** hundreds of spaces, $10 fee
**Distance from car:** short
**Bathrooms:** lots of port-a-potties
**Rentals:** yes
**Boat traffic:** not too bad
**Rating:** ****
**Length:** 6 miles

This is a gorgeous paddle, but like most of Lake Tahoe it can be busy on the weekends, especially along the point between Meeks Bay and Rubicon Bay. Going early is definitely recommended. Not only will the lake be calmer but there will be less boat traffic (although Rubicon Bay is a favorite for early morning water skiers). This section of the lake is fairly close to Emerald Bay so it can get very busy on holidays and weekends.

Meeks Bay Resort (the private section of Meeks Bay) is very easy to paddle from. You can get in as early as 7 the morning — even if the gatehouse is not staffed you can pay the $10 parking fee in the office. There's an easy place to drop off equipment and there's tons of parking. (I don't think it fills up, even on holidays). The beach can get extremely crowded in the summer, but the turquoise water is always gorgeous. There is a marina, though, so you will get boat traffic on busy days.

When you leave the beach, go to the right. The first mile takes you south out of Meeks Bay and down a long point to Rubicon Bay. There are some gorgeous homes on the point, and several times we've seen a seaplane anchored along here.

*Rubicon Bay underwater rocks.*

It's about 3 miles to Lester Beach at D.L. Bliss. Most of the water inside Rubicon Bay is turquoise blue with a few dark rocks peppered around. There are just two "trenches," which seem to be where streams flow into the lake and the water is black and deep. Not only is the water gorgeous, but so are the homes along the shoreline.

It is close to Emerald Bay so you may get a lot of boat traffic on this route. It is best for weekdays or early mornings, although even then you  may see a lot of water skiers.

This is one of the best routes on the west shore with easy access and beautiful water. It's definitely not to be missed.

# 9 - D.L. Bliss to Emerald Bay

**Web:** www.parks.ca.gov
**Phone:** (530) 525-7277
**Parking:** very limited
**Distance from car:** short (at Lester Beach)
**Bathrooms:** yes
**Rentals:** No
**Boat traffic:** can be bad
**Rating:** ****
**Length:** 6 miles

With its steep granite cliffs, this is the most stunning paddle on the lake, but you have to work for it. D.L. Bliss State Park is not close to any of the Tahoe towns and is about 40 minutes south of Tahoe City. Even when you reach the park, it's still a ten minute drive to get to the beach itself. Parking is notoriously difficult and can be full before 9:00 am on weekends and 9:30 on weekdays. There can also be a lot of traffic from boats headed to Emerald Bay. But don't let all of this discourage you. It is absolutely, positively worth it to get up early and make the drive. I promise you won't regret it.

It's important that you park at Lester Beach (or at least go there first to drop off your equipment) as the water can only be reached via a long flight of stairs from the parking lot at Calawee Cove.

Turn right as you head out from the beach. There's a lovely turquoise cove where boats often spend the night, and then the stunning granite cliffs that you pass when hiking the Rubicon Trail. It's a state park so there are no buildings. You'll usually see a few hikers up on the rocks and some osprey (and sometimes even babies in the nest). You may also see a dive boat and bubbles from divers.

*D.L. Bliss State Park.*

This is the deepest shoreline on the lake, with the water reaching depths of a thousand feet just a few hundred feet from the shore. For most of the paddle the water will be jet black because of the depth. It's gorgeous, but also a little creepy.

Because of its proximity to Emerald Bay, there's a fair amount of boat traffic almost every day. Watch the wind because it can kick up quickly and in combination with the boat wakes can get very wavy very fast, and there's nowhere to get out of the water except back at Lester Beach.

# North Shore

The north shore stretches from Carnelian Bay to Sand Harbor. Except for the shoreline just north of Sand Harbor, it's all developed, but the houses are less dense than the developed parts of the west shore and there are far fewer powerboats. It takes just five paddles to complete the north shore but access to some of them can be challenging. Incline Village is closed to non-residents for most of the year. It's hard to find a parking spot at Speedboat Beach and a long walk to the lake even when you do. Despite these challenges, the north shore can be a beautiful and tranquil place to paddle, especially in the fall when Incline is accessible. And Speedboat Beach is not to be missed.

# 10 - Carnelian Bay to Kings Beach

**Web:** www.watermanslanding.com
**Phone:** (530) 546-3590
**Parking:** free spots, street
**Distance from car:** short
**Bathrooms:** yes
**Rentals:** yes
**Boat traffic:** some
**Rating:** **
**Length:** 6 miles

One of the most popular places for renting paddle-boards on Lake Tahoe is Waterman's Landing in Carnelian Bay. Although it's not located on one of Tahoe's premier beaches, it's very convenient. There's a rocky beach that's a short walk from your car and easy to launch from, a cafe, and even clean bathrooms. It's also dog friendly. Between rentals, races, classes, and summer camps Waterman's has been an enthusiastic promoter of paddleboarding on Lake Tahoe, so it's a fitting place to start your tour of the lake.

You'll often see a lot of beginners renting paddle-boards, but you can also demo expensive boards there. They run classes and camps in the summer, but are open year long and some hardy souls paddle all winter long from their beach. I once went in early March and saw several other cold-weather paddlers leave Waterman's that same day.

If the parking at Waterman's is full you can also launch from a little beach that's next to Garwoods (a popular north shore restaurant). It has easy parking, a bathroom, and a little grassy area for drying your board at the end (if you can avoid the goose poop).

At this part of the lake the road runs fairly close to the shore, but there are many beautiful homes. Make a left out of Waterman's and round the point. You can paddle for several miles, passing several resorts and beaches in Agate Bay, including Moondunes, before you reach Kings Beach. Or, if the lake is calm you can take a more direct route across the bay to Kings Beach.

*Carnelian Bay.*

# 11 - Kings Beach to Speedboat Beach

**Web:** www.parks.ca.gov
**Phone:** (530) 583-3074
**Parking:** $10 fee, street
**Distance from car:** short
**Bathrooms**: yes
**Rentals:** yes
**Boat traffic:** ok
**Rating:** ***
**Length:** 6 miles

Although it's fairly nondescript by Tahoe standards (just brown sand, no rocks or pier to swim or jump from), Kings Beach is a very easy place to launch a paddleboard. There are many shops and restaurants, and paddleboard rentals are available at Adrift Surf Shop which is adjacent to the beach. This is a very popular spot for beginners. It's easy to park in the Kings Beach public lot (we often get there as late as 10:15 and there are still tons of spaces available) and just a short walk over sand to the water.

Make a left as you paddle out of the beach and head east toward Nevada. It's shallow and sandy for a mile or so alongside houses and moored boats. After a short time you'll start to see the rocks of Speedboat Beach in the distance. It's about 1-1/2 miles to Speedboat, which is the most dramatic part of the north shore. (See next section.)

If it's a low water year, be extra careful as you paddle around the rocks and into Speedboat Bay as you won't want to hit one with your fin. This is one of Tahoe's most special places and a great place to have a swim or picnic and jump off of the rocks before heading back to Kings Beach.

*Speedboat Beach.*

# 12 - Speedboat Beach to Crystal Bay

**Web:** www.tahoepublicbeaches.com/speedboat-beach/
**Phone:** n/a
**Parking:** very limited street
**Distance from car:** very long with stairs
**Bathrooms:** port-a-potty
**Rentals:** no
**Boat traffic:** ok
**Rating:** ***
**Length:** 6 miles

Speedboat Beach is the jewel of the north shore but a challenging place to paddle from. It's a true "local's beach" with extremely limited parking and a long walk to the shoreline. To get there, you drive toward Nevada from Kings Beach and make the second-to-last right hand turn before the Nevada state line (Speedboat Drive) or the last right hand turn (Harbor Drive) and wind your way down toward the water. If you reach Cal Neva without making the turn, you've missed it, but not by much. When you reach the beach entrance all you will see is a walkway, a sign, and a port-a-potty. Unload your board here and go look for a parking space. It's a long carry down to the water — including a short flight of stairs — but worth every step.

The size of Speedboat Beach varies greatly from year to year, depending on how high the lake is. There's some tension between the beachgoers and the neighbors who claim private property above the high water mark. As a result, in high water level years the beach can be no more than ten feet wide (this is not an exaggeration). But in low years it is hundreds of feet wide and can hold a large crowd.

Paddle out of Speedboat and head left toward Nevada (and away from Kings Beach). You'll pass the private beach of Cal Neva and a couple private homes and then the point that separates Agate Bay from Crystal Bay. The point is deserted and gorgeous. There are beautiful large rocks under water that goes very quickly from turquoise to black as you move out from the shore. In fact, the deepest point in the entire lake is just a little way offshore from the point. It can get choppy at the point almost any time of day as waves from each direction bounce off of it.

You'll pass homes and some deserted cabins and even a little bay that's part of a private resort called Stillwater Cove. When the lake is very calm you can paddle almost directly across the bay to Incline Village. If you continue all the way to where Crystal Bay flattens out along the top of the lake, you'll reach Burnt Cedar Beach, a fabulous private beach in Incline, and an enormous and deserted beach next to it that looks private.

The Incline Beaches are only open to residents for most of the year, so if you want to go ashore (or paddle from them) you'll need to do it in the fall or early spring when they don't check for IDs. Otherwise, it's best to paddle out of Speedboat Beach and enjoy Incline from out on the water.

*Crystal Bay.*

# 13 - Incline Beaches

**Web:** n/a
**Phone:** n/a
**Parking:** residents only
**Distance from car:** short
**Bathrooms:** yes
**Rentals:** no
**Boat traffic:** ok
**Rating:** **
**Length:** 4-1/2 miles

This is one of the more challenging routes to complete if you are trying to paddle the entire lake, but only because of the difficulty of gaining access to the parking lots at the beach. The beaches at Incline are only open to residents (or guests of the Hyatt) for most of the year, so you'll need to go in the fall or spring when they don't check for ID.

Incline Beach is a beautiful sandy beach with tons of tall shade trees. (Only Nevada Beach has as much shade.) It's a very short walk from the car to the beach. If you're trying to link up the entire lake, you'll want to head right from the beach and paddle to Burnt Cedar Beach (or wherever you finished your paddle from Speedboat), then double back and go as far as your endpoint when you paddled north from Sand Harbor (see next section). The water is gorgeous and there are some very large and impressive homes to look at on the shoreline.

If you go in the fall there's virtually no boat traffic. Just stay close to shore if the water is cold.

*Incline Beach.*

# 14 - Sand Harbor to Incline Village

**Web:** parks.nv.gov/parks/sand-harbor/
**Phone:** (775) 831-0494
**Parking:** $12 fee
**Distance from car:** can be long
**Bathrooms:** yes
**Rentals:** yes
**Boat traffic:** ok
**Rating:** ***
**Length:** 4-1/2 miles

Sand Harbor is Lake Tahoe's most popular beach as well as one of the most scenic places to paddle from. It doesn't matter whether you go north or south, both directions are great. Parking can be a little tricky, though, if you haven't been there before. There are three "sections" of the beach. From north to south there's a boat cove to the north, swimming cove in the middle, and long beach on the south. Hard shell boats (including kayaks and paddleboards) are only allowed in the boat cove or the southernmost end of the beach.  Kayak and paddleboard rentals are available at the boat cove, but calling ahead is recommended. Also, the parking lot usually fills by 11:30 on a weekday. Once it fills, it doesn't open again until 3 p.m. so you need to catch a shuttle bus in from Incline.

If you are going to paddle toward Incline, you'll want to park in the most northerly spot available. Call ahead, because if the boat ramp is closed, cars that carry paddleboards or kayaks are allowed to park in the boat launch. Otherwise drop your board at the boat launch, then park at the regular lot and walk back.

*Sand Harbor Boat Cove.*

When you leave the beach, make a right to head north toward Incline. The first part of the paddle will be along state land and you'll pass the turquoise water of Hidden Beach. After awhile, you'll begin to pass beachfront homes (when I went by, there was a lot of construction going on). Try to make it all the way to Incline Beach before you turn back for a total of about 4-½ miles.

# South Shore

Those who are expecting mobs of people, a highly developed shoreline, and an Atlantic City-style experience will be pleasantly surprised by the south shore. Stretching from Emerald Bay to Nevada Beach, it includes some golden marshy shoreline and turquoise water that's unlike any other part of the lake. Emerald Bay is the most famous spot on the lake, but head the other direction for an equally lovely paddle. The strip malls and casinos and crowds that you see when driving through South Lake are largely invisible from the water, and only two of the paddles are in front of highly developed areas. South shore paddling is easily accessible and this part of the lake takes just five outings to complete.

# 15 - Emerald Bay

**Web:** www.parks.ca.gov
**Phone:** (530) 525-7232
**Parking:** 50 spaces, $10 fee
**Distance from car:** 1 mile, renting is a must
**Bathrooms:** yes
**Rentals:** yes
**Boat traffic:** very heavy
**Rating:** ****
**Length:** 4 miles

Parking at Emerald Bay can be a challenge. There are only about 50 spots in the lot, and they often fill up early, even on weekdays. Read the signs carefully if you park on the street, as this is a favorite place for the police to give tickets.

You can do Emerald Bay as part of an 8 mile paddle from Baldwin Beach (or a really long paddle from D.L. Bliss State Park, which I don't recommend due to boat traffic) or hike down from the road and rent a paddleboard on the beach. It's a steep one-mile hike down to Emerald from the parking lot so carrying your board is not an option. If you hike into Emerald Bay you can also tour the Vikingsholm mansion after your paddle. There are plenty of bathrooms and you can also purchase snacks.

Rentals are available from West Shore Sports. The shop opens at 10 and reservations are highly recommended. Your best bet if renting is to try to get on the water right at 10 so you avoid the wind that can kick up starting at 11.

There are usually a lot of boats in Emerald Bay but there is a 15 knot restriction so the waves aren't too terrible. You'll want to keep an eye out for the M.S. Dixie which visits from Zephyr Cove a few times a day and kicks up a big wake.

The south side of Emerald Bay is very wild. We saw 5 osprey nests and several kingfishers. There is also a submerged dock that is a favorite for divers. There was only one boat moored along this side when we visited.

*Emerald Bay's south shore.*

The mouth of the Bay has shallow, turquoise water but crossing it can be challenging. Even early in the morning it is congested and sometimes crazy people will pull tubes or water skiers right to the entrance, with no regard for kayaks or boarders. Your best bet is to wait until there are no boats coming and then paddle like mad to get across.

On the north shore there are campgrounds and several lovely little beaches that are a short walk from the main beach. You'll often see boats moored along this shore. You can also paddle to Fannette Island with its stone tea house. Unbelievably, it's the only island in the entire lake. This is one of the most iconic places in Tahoe and not to be missed.

# 16 - Baldwin Beach to Emerald Bay

**Web:** www.tahoepublicbeaches.com/baldwin-beach/
**Phone:** n/a
**Parking:** tons, $8 fee
**Distance from car:** short
**Bathrooms:** yes
**Rentals:** yes
**Boat traffic:** heavy
**Rating:** ****
**Length:** 4 miles

Baldwin Beach, a few steep, winding miles from Emerald Bay, is a lovely place to paddle. It's probably the best launching spot on the south shore, with a sandy beach, turquoise water, and the easy access to Emerald Bay. Unfortunately, because it is close to Emerald Bay there can be a lot of boat traffic. Your best bet is to go on a weekday, but if you need to go on a weekend be sure to go very early. You'll see other paddleboarders, kayakers, and probably some water skiers.

It's easy to get into the water at Baldwin. Rentals are available from Kayak Tahoe (reserving ahead is recommended.) If you turn left out of the beach and head up the west shore you'll pass a few homes and then wild land on the way to Emerald Bay. It's very beautiful. The entrance to Emerald Bay spans between two buoys. Be careful of boat traffic when you are near the entrance of the bay. It can be very congested and you frequently see boaters that are going much faster than they should. You can turn into the bay or cross the entrance and paddle up along the wild shore of D.L. Bliss State Park. The complete paddle is 4 miles, but if you add Emerald Bay it's 8.

*Baldwin Beach from Emerald Bay.*

# 17 - Baldwin Beach to Pope Beach

**Web:** www.tahoepublicbeaches.com/baldwin-beach/
**Phone:** n/a
**Parking:** plenty, $8 fee
**Distance from car:** short
**Bathrooms:** yes
**Rentals:** yes
**Boat traffic:** can be bad
**Rating:** ****
**Length:** 8 miles

Baldwin Beach, a few steep, winding miles from Emerald Bay, is a lovely place to paddle. It's probably the best launching spot on the south shore, with a easy access and turquoise water. Unfortunately, because it is close to Emerald Bay there is can be a lot of boat traffic. Your best bet is to go on a weekday, but if you need to go on a weekend be sure to go very early. You'll probably see other paddleboarders, kayakers, and water skiers.

Most people make Emerald Bay their destination out of Baldwin but if you make a right out of the beach you can paddle past long, beautiful stretches of undeveloped land. You'll pass the marshes at Kiva Shoreline and dog-friendly Tallac Shoreline (pull in if you want to see Tallac Mansion) before you encounter the marina and houses of Camp Richardson. It's definitely one of the loveliest stretches of Lake Tahoe, although in a less dramatic way than Sand Harbor and D.L. Bliss. If you keep going past Camp Richardson you'll reach beautiful, marshy Pope Beach where you can turn around. You can easily put in at any time along the way, and there's even a restaurant at Camp Richardson if you want to stop for a snack or meal.

*Baldwin Beach.*

# 18 - Pope Beach to Connolly Beach

**Web:** www.tahoesbest.com/pope-beach
**Phone:** 530-543-2600
**Parking:** plenty, $8 fee
**Distance from car:** Not bad
**Bathrooms:** yes
**Rentals:** yes
**Boat traffic:** Not bad
**Rating:** *
**Length:** 7 miles

Pope Beach is ¾ miles long and just 3 miles from South Lake Tahoe on Highway 89. It has hundreds of parking spots, a concession stand, and paddleboard and kayak rentals. It's a great place to launch for a south Tahoe paddle. (Although Tahoe Keys just to the east is not officially open to the public, it's also easy to launch there.)

To get to Connolly you need to make a right when you paddle out of Pope Beach and head toward South Lake and Heavenly ski area. You'll pass the canals of Tahoe Keys, then the Upper Truckee marsh. After that, the paddle becomes less interesting as you pass a lot of condos and South Lake development. You'll pass Reagan and EL Dorado beaches before reaching Connolly (a public beach which is part of the Best Western Timber Cove Lodge and Marina). This paddle is only recommended if you are trying to link up the lake. If you are just looking for a paddle from Pope Beach, go left instead and paddle toward Baldwin Beach for some gorgeous scenery.

*Upper Truckee Marsh.*

# 19 - Nevada Beach to Connolly Beach

**Web:** www.tahoepublicbeaches.com/nevada-beach/
**Phone:** (775) 588-5562
**Parking:** Easy midweek/busy weekends, $7
**Distance from car:** not bad
**Bathrooms:** yes
**Rentals:** yes
**Boat traffic:** not bad
**Rating:** ***
**Length:** 6 miles

You wouldn't know it from the road, but the south shore is really gorgeous. Nevada Beach is a big, deserty beach a half mile long and 300 feet wide with lots of trees. We typically wouldn't drive from the west shore past Sand Harbor — or Bliss or Baldwin for that matter — to go there, but it is very lovely, and its proximity to the casinos makes it a great option for South Lake visitors. I went mid-week and it was fairly deserted (except, apparently, for the person that stole my flip flops while I was out on the water), but we've seen huge lines of cars trying to get in on weekends. Because this beach is lovelier and easier to paddle from, I've switched direction so you'll need to paddle back to Connelly Beach to link up the lake.

*Nevada Beach.*

The route is gorgeous. The lake here is shallow (especially in dry years) so the water is turquoise. South Lake is known for its casinos, so you might expect to see an Atlantic City-style beachfront but it's actually very mellow and wild. Heading south from Nevada Beach you pass a golf course and then some lowkey private homes (not over the top at all). There are a few places— like where the Tahoe Queen goes out — that look a bit touristy, and you'll probably see a parasail boat and jetskis, but otherwise not too much traffic. Nevada Beach is very easy to go out of, with a shortish walk from the car, bathrooms, picnic tables, and even a tiny snack shack.

# East Shore

The east shore stretches from Nevada Beach in south shore up to Sand Harbor. It's the least developed part of the lake, the most dramatic, and the hardest to access. Save this part for last so you can train for the longer legs. You'll need to do some lengthy paddles to complete it, but you won't want to miss any of it. Depending on how you break the shore up, you can finish this part of the lake in five paddles or less. But you may need some assistance from a friend to either pick you up on a boat, or help you drop a car. The dramatic rocks of Sand Harbor, the vibrant turquoise waters of Secret Beach, the deserted coast of Deadman's Point — these are all highlights of the east shore that you won't want to miss.

# 20 - Nevada Beach to Zephyr Cove

**Web:** www.tahoepublicbeaches.com/nevada-beach/
**Phone:** (775) 588-5562
**Parking:** Easy midweek/busy weekends, $7
**Distance from car:** not bad
**Bathrooms:** yes
**Rentals:** yes
**Boat traffic:** not bad
**Rating:** ***
**Length:** 4-½ miles

In all the times I drove through South Shore, I never realized how beautiful it was until I saw Baldwin and Nevada Beaches. Nevada is a big, deserty beach almost a mile long and 300 feet wide with lots of trees. The paddle between Nevada Beach and Zephyr Cove is lovely. You'll see interesting rocks, turquoise water, and some beautiful homes.

As you paddle out of the beach, turn right to head north to Zephyr Cove. It can be wavy at the start but after you round the rocky point you'll be at Round Hill Pines, a quiet public beach (and the home of the Lake Tahoe Bleu Wave, a hip 1966 yacht that takes tourists to Emerald Bay). There's a long bay and then a long flat point before you round the corner to Zephyr Cove. There are a number of homes along the south part of Zephyr Cove but paddle all the way to the beach, which can be very lively on weekends or holidays. There's even a snack bar there if you're hungry.

You can see Heavenly the whole way back but it's not until you round the point below Round Hill that you can see the casinos beyond Nevada Beach. They look surprisingly small from the water.

*Heavenly from Round Hill Pines.*

# 21 - Zephyr Cove to Cave Rock

**Web:** www.zephyrcove.com/
**Phone:** 775-589-4907
**Parking:** plenty, $8 fee
**Distance from car:** short
**Bathrooms:** yes
**Rentals:** yes
**Boat traffic:** not bad
**Rating:** ***
**Length:** 4-1/2

If you are driving to Zephyr Cove from Tahoe City, it's exactly the same distance whether you go around the north lake or south, but I highly recommend going via Incline as the traffic in South Lake can be unimaginably bad in the summer. Without traffic it's an hour either way.

Zephyr Cove is an easy place to launch from. It's a privately run resort — like Meeks Bay — with a beach, cabins, watercraft rentals, restaurant, and more. The M.S. Dixie even leaves from there for its Emerald Bay cruises. The beach can be crowded and raucous at times, but it's easy to park there early in the morning and only a short walk to get your board to the water.

Make a right out of the beach to go north to Cave Rock. It's a lovely paddle with turquoise water, pretty homes, and interesting rock formations. Cave Rock is a dramatic destination just two miles north. There's a little beach on the south side of Cave Rock park where you can pull in if you want a rest (or to use the bathroom). Because Cave Rock is primarily a boat launch, it's best to do this paddle early, on a weekday, or both.

*Cave Rock.*

# 22 - Cave Rock to Glenbrook

**Web:** www.tahoepublicbeaches.com/cave-rock/
**Phone:** (775) 588-7975
**Parking:** 40 spaces, $8 fee
**Distance from car:** short
**Bathrooms:** yes
**Rentals:** no
**Boat traffic:** can be bad
**Rating:** ***
**Length:** 7 miles

If you drive south from Sand Harbor (Highway 28 to 50), Cave Rock is the first public place where you can easily launch a paddleboard — about 13 miles down the road. In order to paddle this side of the lake you need to either travel that entire distance in one, long paddle (13 miles one way) or find a way to get out at Glenbrook or one of the adjoining neighborhoods. I'm treating this distance as three separate there-and-back paddles: Cave Rock to Glenbrook, Glenbrook to Secret Harbor, and Sand Harbor to Secret Harbor. If you can't figure out a way to launch from Glenbrook (see next entry), start very, very early in the morning from Cave Rock and bring a lunch so you can get all the way to Sand Harbor in one day. (The wind most often comes from the south, so it's better to start at Cave Rock). If, for some reason, you weren't able to finish, you could walk up to the road from Skunk Harbor (1 mile) or Chimney Beach (½ mile) but it would be difficult to get your board out.

Cave Rock Park is a small day-use area that's tucked beneath the rugged volcanic face of Cave Rock. There are 40 parking spots and a boat launch ramp, dock, restroom, and a very tiny beach on the south end. Other than the little beach, it's very rocky and there's not an easy way in or out of the water. There's really no reason to come here unless you are launching a powerboat or going for a paddle. But the paddling from Cave Rock is very nice.

When you head out of the beach, turn right and paddle north. If it's a low water year, watch out for boulders just beneath the surface as you paddle along the Cave Rock parking area and boat launch. Keep an eye out for boats as you pass the launch at the north end of the park. Cave Rock itself is right after the launch. In the morning, it casts a long shadow on the water, which is dark and creepy. But immediately after you pass the rock you'll find shallow turquoise water. You'll see homes, beaches, and something that looks like a church camp, intermittently along this shoreline. There are also stretches of undeveloped land. The only downside is that there you can hear the road for most of the paddle.

You'll reach an area called Logan Shoals where there are a lot of above-water and underwater rocks to navigate around. (There's a viewpoint from the road if you want to look down on this area before paddling). After the rocks, you'll reach the south end of Glenbrook Bay. As you round the point you'll see some very large homes

on the rocky hillside and then the long sandy stretch of
Glenbrook Beach.

# 23 - Glenbrook to Whale Beach

**Web:** glenbrooktahoe.org
**Phone:** (775) 749-526
**Parking:** No parking
**Distance from car:** n/a
**Bathrooms:** n/a
**Rentals:** No
**Boat traffic:** ok
**Rating:** ****
**Length:** 10 miles

It's about 13 miles along the shore between Sand Harbor and Cave Rock (longer by car). This book divides the distance into three paddles - Cave Rock to Glenbrook, Glenbrook to Secret Harbor, and Sand Harbor to Secret Harbor. But don't try to launch from Glenbrook without making plans in advance as it is a gated community and you won't be able to get in. Try to call the homeowners association or arrive by boat. Your alternative is to do a lengthy one-way paddle from Cave Rock to Sand Harbor. It's a long way, but it's also the biggest stretch of undeveloped land on the whole lake, the most deserted, and the most beautiful part of the lake.

Glenbrook is a sandy bay with a beach that's about a mile long and lots of beautiful homes along the shore. When you leave Glenbrook beach, turn right (north) and in minutes you'll be paddling along undeveloped shore.

We passed one little home with a couple of kayaks pulled up on the shore, and a couple of tents, but the rest was deserted. There's almost no boat traffic along this part of the shore. We did see one early fisherman who pulled an 18 inch fish out of the lake while we were watching — the only live fish I've ever seen on Lake Tahoe.

*Deadman Point.*

It's a couple of miles before you get all the way around Deadman Point to the north of Glenbrook. It's a long flat point with beautiful rocks and an osprey nest or two. After another mile or so, you reach Skunk Harbor where you may see a few boats camped out. Skunk Harbor is at least a mile from the road, so there aren't a ton of beachgoers, but it's a historic site, and you can see the remains of some old buildings if you paddle into the bay. (If you're doing a long paddle and want to save time, stay deep and don't go into the bay.)

*Skunk Harbor.*

Past Skunk Harbor you'll reach Secret Harbor with its beautiful rock formations and bright blue water. This is probably the most beautiful spot on all of Lake Tahoe. There are a few homes along the south shore of the bay that seem only to be accessible by boat. They have private beach signs on the docks, but the rest of the beaches are public. It's less than a mile from the road so you may encounter people on the beach with their dogs. (The beaches in Nevada are dog-friendly.) The Secret Beach cove is locally known as a nude beach, so you may also see scenery of a different type. Expect to see some mo-torboats, and maybe some water skiers, but not as much boat traffic as you would on the west shore.

# 24 - Sand Harbor to Secret Harbor

**Web:** parks.nv.gov/parks/sand-harbor/
**Phone:** (775) 831-0494
**Parking:** Lots, $12 fee
**Distance from car:** varies
**Bathrooms:** yes
**Rentals:** yes
**Boat traffic:** ok
**Rating:** ****
**Length:** 8-1/2 miles

This is one of the most beautiful paddles on Lake Tahoe. For an easier start, leave from the south end of Sand Harbor (the farthest point from the boat beach). It's a short walk from the car to the water and there are bathrooms, but a long way from the snack bar.

Turn left out of the beach and head south. After a mile or so you pass a tiny cove with a little turquoise beach and the Thunderbird Lodge. (You may even get to see the lodge's beautiful wood boat.) You'll then need to paddle along a long rocky point that can feel very exposed with lots of waves, until you hit Chimney Beach. You'll recognize it by the chimney that's literally standing on its own in the middle of the beach. The water there is calmer and very turquoise. It's only a half a mile from Chimney Beach up to the road, so you'll probably see a lot of beachgoers and dogs on the shore. (The Nevada shore is dog-friendly.) It's another half a mile to Secret Beach, Secret

Harbor, and Whale Beach. The water was really shallow when we paddled this way and we saw several rocks a long way from shore with fresh propeller marks. These beaches are less than a mile from the road so you'll see lots of beachgoers, often with their dogs. Secret Harbor is known by the locals as a nude beach, so you may see scenery of a different kind.

At Whale Beach there are some homes which seem to be only accessible by boat. They range from tiny shack to luxurious lake house. There's even what appears to be a permanent tent. (All have "Private Beach" signs.) Because of it's proximity to Sand Harbor, you will get some boat traffic, but nothing like the west shore.

*Secret Beach.*

# Extra long paddle routes

If you want to try a day-long excursion, Tahoe has some excellent long distance options. You'll need to do some advanced planning to either leave a car at one end or have a friend pick you up. Be sure to check the weather so you know in advance if it will be windy in the afternoon. And bring plenty of water and food.

### Chambers Landing to D.L. Bliss (one way)

This west shore gem takes you by Sugar Pine Point, Meeks Bay, and into Rubicon Bay. The only trick is that if parking is full at D.L. Bliss it might be difficult to coordinate a ride.

### D.L. Bliss to Emerald Bay (and back)

If you get an early start from Lester Beach at D.L. Bliss you can paddle to Emerald Bay, circle the bay, and then head back. The wind often blows from the south, so it would be at your back for the trip home. It could be very choppy, though, if there's a lot of boat traffic.

### Cave Rock to Sand Harbor (one way)

If you want a long paddle, this is your best bet. This 13 mile route includes the stretch between Glenbrook and Sand Harbor which is the most beautiful part of the lake.

There aren't any good places to get out between Glen-brook and Sand Harbor, though, so be prepared and check the wind in advance. If you start from Cave Rock, you will be only a third of the way to your destination when you enter the point where you can't easily exit.

# Dog-friendly beaches

Many people love to paddle with their pooches. There are plenty of places in Tahoe where you can take your dog for a swim or paddle. Be sure to check the signs for the latest restrictions, but these beaches all seem to be dog-friendly.

**North shore**
- Coon Street Beach in Kings Beach - dogs allowed.
- Waterman's Landing and adjacent Patton Beach – dogs allowed.

**West shore**
- Sugar Pine Point – only allows dogs on leashes, but we've seen plenty off-leash dogs there.
- Hurricane Bay - you can also take dogs on the rocky shoreline along 89.
- Lakeshore Beach - seems to have a lot of four-legged visitors.

**South shore**
- Kiva Beach - allows off leash dogs.

**East shore**
- Zephyr Cove - has a dog-friendly area.

- Chimney Beach - allows off leash dogs but you need to hike or paddle in.
- Secret Harbor - allows off leash dogs but you need to hike or paddle in.
- Skunk Harbor - allows off leash dogs but you need to hike or paddle in.

*Paddling on the west shore with my dog, Sherwood.*

# Where to rent or buy

These are just a few of the many options for renting or buying paddleboards around Lake Tahoe. You can rent one at the beach, or strap it on your car if you want to explore. Some places will even deliver one to you at the location of your choice. Paddleboarding has grown in popularity over the past few years so be sure to reserve ahead in the summertime.

Waterman's Landing
www.watermanslanding.com
(530) 546-3590
Rentals start at $25/hour ($80/day) for standard boards and $35/hour for high performance demo boards.

Tahoe City Kayak
www.tahoecitykayak.com
(530) 581-4336
Rent at Commons Beach in Tahoe City and Sand Harbor (or call and request delivery)
Rates run from $25/hour to $75/day.

West Shore Sports
www.westshoresports.com
(530) 525-9920
Rent at Homewood, Sunnyside, and Sugar Pine Point.

Rates start at $20/hour. West shore deliveries are also available.


Adrift
www.standuppaddletahoe.com
530-546-4112
Shop is adjacent to Kings Beach State Park. Rates start at $20/hour.


Kayak Tahoe
www.kayaktahoe.com
(530) 544-2011
Rent at Nevada, Pope, and Baldwin Beaches, Emerald Bay, or the Timber Cove Marina in South Lake. Rates run from $20/hour to $65/day.


Action Watersports
(530) 525-5588
www.action-watersports.com
Rent at Camp Richardson, Meeks Bay Marina, and Timber Cove and Lakeside Marinas in South Lake. Rates start at $30/hour.

## ABOUT THE AUTHOR

Laura Norman spends her summers near the west shore in Lake Tahoe. Over the past five years, she's explored every inch of the lake on her Tahoe SUP paddleboard. When she's not out on the water, she does content marketing for a large technology company. She lives in San Francisco with her husband, two children, and Portuguese water dog, Sherwood.